Published By Robert Corbin

VEGAN DIET

Delicious Recipes and Practical Advice for Living a Plant-based Lifestyle

Published By Robert Corbin

@ Daryl Meis

Vegan Diet: Delicious Recipes and Practical

Advice for Living a Plant-based Lifestyle

All Right RESERVED

ISBN 978-87-94477-93-2

TABLE OF CONTENTS

Minced Tempeh Salad 1

Vegan "Chicken" Salad 5

Vegan Cassoulet 7

Vanilla Fig Oatmeal Topped With Baklava Filling 10

Vanilla Fig Oatmeal 11

Mango Tofu Tacos 14

Shakshuka 17

Harass 19

Vegan Bagels 21

Quiche Breakfast Cups 23

Mediterranean Breakfast Burrito 25

Tofu Avocado Toast 27

Apple Buckwheat Pancakes 29

Mediterranean Chickpeas On Toast 32

Applesauce Muffins 33

Whole Wheat Raisin Bread 35

Orange Raspberry Muffins 37

Kidney-Supportive Salads Quinoa And Vegetable Salad 39

Kale And White Bean Salad 41

Spinach And Beet Salad 43

Vegan Spinach And Artichoke Dip 45

Vegan Mushroom And Lentil Bolognese 49

Vegan Avocado And Chickpea Salad Sandwich 53

Quinoa And Black Bean Fiesta Salad 56

Faro And Roasted Vegetable Salad 58

Brown Rice And Edam Me Salad 60

Shoyu Ramen With Teriyaki Glazed Eggplant 61

Ginger-Sesame Shoyu Ramen With Crispy Tofu 63

Lemongrass-Infused Shout Ramen 65

Creamy Avocado Spread 67

Kid-Friendly Guacamole 69

Easy Homemade Vegan Cheese Dip 71

Banana Quinoa Oatmeal 73

Gingerbread Chia Porridge 75

Roasted Balsamic Brussels Sprouts 77

Quinoa Primavera	79
Creamy Cashew Cheese Sauce	82
Vegan Tofu And Vegetable Wrap	84
Vegan Poke Bowl	86
Vegan Taco Bowl	88
Cauliflower Hash Browns	90
Flaxseed And Berry Muffins	92
Vegan Keto Breakfast Burrito	94
Brown Rice And Lentils	96
Instant Pot Black Eyed Peas	98
Pot Vegan Baked Beans	100
Cajun Corn And Kidney Bean Salad	103
Arugula Lentil Salad	105
Kale Salad With Grilled Eggplant	107
Tofu Vegetable Kebabs	111
Braised Lentils	114
Polenta With Mushrooms	117
Cinnamon Walnut Porridge	120

Banana Blueberry Breakfast Muffin 122

Cauliflower Fried Rice 124

Ginger Cinnamon Waffles 126

Easy Vegan French Toast 129

Artichoke Spinach Quiche 131

Cranberry Muffins 134

Apple Cinnamon Muffins 136

Minced Tempeh Salad

Ingredients:

- 1 tbsp chopped mint
- 1 tbsp chopped coriander (cilantro)
- 1-2 spring onions, cut into thick slices
- Vegetable or peanut oil, for frying
- 5 small Asian shallots, sliced thinly (about 2 tablespoons)
- 2-3 cloves garlic, sliced thinly (about 1 tablespoon)
- handful of cashews
- 2 stalks lemongrass, tough outer layer removed, minced
- 2 tsp palm or light brown sugar
- 2 tsp toasted sesame seeds

- 2 tsp soy sauce
- 1 tsp fresh lime juice
- Fresh lime, for garnish (optional)

Tempeh

- 1 1/2 teaspoons tamarind concentrate
- 1 tsp palm or light brown sugar
- 1 tsp soy sauce
- 1 tsp sri racha
- 105 grams (3/4 cup) tempeh in 1/4 inch cubes
- 1 tbsp rice flour

Directions:

1. Heat about 1/2 an inch of oil to medium heat in a large skillet or frying pan. Line a large plate (or two) with paper towels.
2. In a separate small bowl, combine the salad INGREDIENTS: up to and including the spring onions.

3. To begin the frying process, add the cashews to the oil and fry for 1-2 minutes, or until lightly golden. Remove with a slotted spoon to drain on the paper towels.
4. Follow with the shallots, which you'll need to fry for 1/2 minutes, until just turning brown but not burnt. Remove as above. Fry the garlic in the same manner for 30 seconds (absolutely do not let burn). Remove and place on the paper towels.

Tempeh

5. Stir the tamarind, sugar, soy sauce, sri racha together in a medium bowl. Add the tempeh and mix through to soak up the liquid. Tip in the rice flour and toss to coat the tempeh evenly.
6. Tip in the tempeh mixture into the oil, stirring frequently to ensure it's evenly fried. After 4-5 minutes the tempeh will be crispy and a deep

golden brown. Remove it with the slotted spoon and place on the paper towels.

7. To put the salad together you can plate the individual components seperately or combine everything; that's down to personal preference (as is whether you choose to eat it hot or cold). Serve with sri racha and/or thin slices of fresh chili and a slice of lime.

3. To begin the frying process, add the cashews to the oil and fry for 1-2 minutes, or until lightly golden. Remove with a slotted spoon to drain on the paper towels.
4. Follow with the shallots, which you'll need to fry for 1/2 minutes, until just turning brown but not burnt. Remove as above. Fry the garlic in the same manner for 30 seconds (absolutely do not let burn). Remove and place on the paper towels.

Tempeh

5. Stir the tamarind, sugar, soy sauce, sri racha together in a medium bowl. Add the tempeh and mix through to soak up the liquid. Tip in the rice flour and toss to coat the tempeh evenly.
6. Tip in the tempeh mixture into the oil, stirring frequently to ensure it's evenly fried. After 4-5 minutes the tempeh will be crispy and a deep

golden brown. Remove it with the slotted spoon and place on the paper towels.

7. To put the salad together you can plate the individual components seperately or combine everything; that's down to personal preference (as is whether you choose to eat it hot or cold). Serve with sri racha and/or thin slices of fresh chili and a slice of lime.

Vegan "Chicken" Salad

Ingredients:

- As much pepper as you like
- Two avocados
- One package of textured soy protein (Lightlife Smart Strips are delicious)
- 1 cup of chopped celery
- ½ cup of chopped onions
- ½ cup of sliced almonds
- ¼ cup of flax seeds
- ¾ cup of Veganese
- 1 ½ cups of halved red grapes
- Splash of lemon juice
- One head of green leaf lettuce

Directions:

1. Place all of the INGREDIENTS:, except the avocados and lettuce, into a large bowl and mix.
2. Take four plates, place desired amount of lettuce on to each, and then add two large spoonfuls of your delicious Vegan "Chicken" Salad.
3. Slice half of an avocado on to each plate.
4. Enjoy!

Vegan Cassoulet

Ingredients:

- 2 cups pre-cooked field peas or black-eyed peas(feel free to just use 1 1/2 cups if you are using canned peas)

- 1 1/2 cups diced tomatoes (or a 14.5 ounce can – do not drain)

- 1 1/2 cups chicken seitan (or about 2 packages Lightlife Smart Strips), chopped

- 1 to 2 cups water plus 1 tablespoon vegan chick'n bouillon(or same amount broth, it can be from the seitan if you are using homemade)

- 2 bay leaves

- 1 sprig rosemary

- 1 tablespoon Herbs de Provence

- 1 teaspoon thyme
- 1/2 teaspoon liquid smoke or smoked paprika (or 1/2 teaspoon smoked salt and no additional salt)
- 1 small onion, minced
- 1/2 tube Lightlife Gimme Lean sausage (or your favorite sausage crumbles)
- 2 stalks celery, chopped
- 3 small carrots, chopped
- salt to taste

Directions:

1. The night before: Heat a pan over medium heat then add the onion, a few tablespoons water and sauté until translucent. Add the Gimme Lean to the onion mixture in the pan.
2. Cook until you can crumble the sausage easily with your spatula and it is browned and cooked thoroughly.

3. Chop the celery and carrots. Store everything together in the fridge overnight.
4. In the morning: Add everything to the slow cooker to an oiled slow cooker. Cook on low for 6 to 8 hours. Remove rosemary stem then serve.

Vanilla Fig Oatmeal Topped With Baklava Filling

Ingredients:

- 1/4 teaspoon cardamom
- 1/4 teaspoon food grade orange flower water (optional)
- 1/2 vanilla bean scraped or 1/2 teaspoon vanilla paste or 1 teaspoon vanilla
- 1 tablespoon chopped pistachios
- 1 tablespoon chopped walnuts
- 1 tablespoon chopped almonds
- 1 tablespoon brown rice syrup
- 1/2 cup steel-cut oats
- 2 cups unsweetened So Delicious Coconut Milk (only 50 calories a cup!)
- 1/2 cup chopped dried figs

- 1 tablespoon agave nectar
- pinch of cinnamon

Directions:

1. The night before: Spray your crock with some oil to help with clean up later. Add everything except baklava filling topping INGREDIENTS: to the slow cooker.
2. Now mix together the 'baklava filling' in a small bowl and store in the fridge until the morning. Cook on low over night (7 to 9 hours).
3. In the morning: Stir your oatmeal well. It may seem watery at the top but if stirred it should become a more uniform consistency.
4. Top each serving with a few tablespoons of the baklava filling, making it as sweet as you like it.

Vanilla Fig Oatmeal

Ingredients:

- 1/4 teaspoon food grade orange flower water (optional)
- 1/2 vanilla bean scraped or 1/2 teaspoon vanilla paste or 1 teaspoon vanilla
- 1 tablespoon chopped pistachios
- 1 tablespoon chopped walnuts
- 1 tablespoon chopped almonds
- 1 tablespoon brown rice syrup
- 1/2 cup steel-cut oats
- 2 cups unsweetened So Delicious Coconut Milk (only 50 calories a cup!)
- 1/2 cup chopped dried figs
- 1/4 teaspoon cardamom
- 1 tablespoon agave nectar
- pinch of cinnamon

Directions:

1. The night before: Spray your crock with some oil to help with clean up later.
2. Add everything except baklava filling topping INGREDIENTS: to the slow cooker.
3. Now mix together the 'baklava filling' in a small bowl and store in the fridge until the morning. Cook on low over night (7 to 9 hours).
4. In the morning: Stir your oatmeal well. It may seem watery at the top but if stirred it should become a more uniform consistency.
5. Top each serving with a few tablespoons of the baklava filling, making it as sweet as you like it.

Mango Tofu Tacos

Ingredients:

For the Baked Tofu:

- 1/2 tsp garlic powder
- 1/2 tsp crushed black pepper
- 1 tsp olive oil
- 1/2 of 1 14-ounce package firm tofu
- 1 tsp cumin powder
- 1 tsp cayenne
- 1 tsp sea salt

For the Mango Salsa:

- 1/2 cup diced mango
- 1 tbsp. chopped red onion
- 1/2 of 1 jalapeño, seeded and finely diced
- 1 fresh basil leaf, torn

For the Spicy Guacamole:

- 1/2 of 1 jalapeño, seeded and finely diced
- A pinch of cilantro, chopped finely
- Juice from 1 lime
- 1 tsp salt
- 1 avocado

Directions:
1. Preheat oven to 350°F and line a baking tray with parchment paper.
2. Cut the tofu into thin strips and then cut those into triangles, as shown.
3. Combine cumin, cayenne, salt, garlic powder, pepper, and olive oil in a small bowl.
4. Drizzle over tofu until evenly coated and place tofu on baking sheet.
5. Bake for 15 minutes, flipping halfway through cooking. Let cool on a wire rack.

6. In a separate bowl, combine diced mango, finely chopped red onion, half of the jalapeño, and basil.
7. Mix well and set aside.
8. On a chopping board, combine jalapeño and cilantro.
9. Mash avocado with a fork over the jalapeño and cilantro.
10. Add lime juice and salt and mash further.
11. If desired, warm tortillas on a dry pan over medium heat.
12. To assemble, add 2-3 pieces of tofu to a taco and top with 1 tablespoon mango mixture and 1 tablespoon guacamole.
13. Serve with additional cilantro, if desired.

Shakshuka

Ingredients:

- 1 tsp cumin
- 2-3 tbsp. harissa (The next recipe)
- 2 tbsp. tomato purée
- 1 14.5-ounce can chopped tomatoes
- Salt and pepper, to taste
- 1 14-ounce package silken tofu
- 2 tsp olive oil
- 1 white or red onion
- 6 garlic cloves
- 2 red peppers
- 1 tsp each paprika, turmeric, and cayenne pepper to season the tofu

Directions:

1. If making the harissa from scratch, do this first.
2. Heat the olive oil in a large frying pan or skillet over medium heat.
3. Slice the onions and garlic and chop the red peppers, discarding the seeds.
4. Add these to the pan and stir to coat in the oil, followed by the cumin, harissa, and tomato purée.
5. Cook for about 5 minutes, until the onions begin to soften.
6. Now stir in the chopped tomatoes, salt, and pepper and then leave for around 15 minutes.
7. While this is cooking, drain the tofu and lightly mash it in a bowl. If using, stir in the paprika, turmeric, and cayenne pepper.
8. 5 minutes before serving, add the tofu to the shakshuka. You can stir it in as much as you like, or leave it on top.

Harass

Ingredients:

- 4 cloves of garlic
- 1 tsp salt
- 3 tbsp. olive oil
- ¼ cup fresh cilantro
- ¼ cup dried red cayenne peppers
- 20 mild red chilies such as the Byadgi or Ancho Chilies (also Dried)
- 1 1/2 tbsp. cumin seeds
- 1 tsp coriander seeds
- 1 tbsp. chopped mint (optional)

Directions:

1. Soak the chilies with ½ cup warm water for 15 minutes.

2. Drain and reserve the water.
3. In the meantime, toast the cumin and coriander seeds.
4. Grind to a powder in a coffee grinder.
5. Place the chilies, ground spices, garlic, salt and olive oil with a little water in a blender and grind to a paste.
6. Add in the chopped cilantro and the mint and pulse a few times.
7. Use some more water if needed.
8. Store the mixture in the refrigerator and use as needed.

Vegan Bagels

Ingredients:

- Cold water, 1 cup
- Ground psyllium husks, ¼ cup
- Salt, ¼ teaspoon
- Ground flaxseed, ½ cup
- Tahini, ½ cup
- Baking powder, 1 teaspoon

Directions:

1. Heat the oven to 375 F.
2. Lay aluminum foil or parchment paper over a baking sheet.
3. Blend in a medium-sized mixing bowl the flax seeds, psyllium husks, salt, and baking powder.
4. In a small bowl, blend the water into the tahini.

5. Pour the water and tahini into the seed mixture and blend them into a ball of dough.
6. Put the dough ball out onto the counter and separate it into six dough lumps of equal size.
7. Roll the dough into round balls.
8. Flatten the dough balls into patties about ¼ inches thick.
9. Lay the dough patties onto the baking pan.
10. Cut out the center with a small round object.
11. Bake the bagels for forty-five minutes, or they turn golden brown.

Quiche Breakfast Cups

Ingredients:

- Nutritional yeast, ½ cup
- Extra-firm tofu, one block
- Canned tomato paste, 1 tablespoon
- Water, 3 tablespoons
- Lemon juice, 1 tablespoon
- Dijon mustard, 2 tablespoons
- Cornstarch, 1 tablespoon
- Garlic powder, 2 teaspoons
- Frozen spinach, thawed, 4 cups

Directions:
1. Heat the oven to 350 F.
2. Put paper liner cups into a muffin pan with twelve cups.

3. Put everything into a blender except the spinach. Blend this mixture on high until it is creamy and smooth.
4. Divide the spinach evenly in the twelve muffin cups.
5. Pour the blender mixture into the muffin papers on top of the spinach.
6. Bake the muffins for 30 minutes.

Mediterranean Breakfast Burrito

Ingredients:

- Sliced black olives, 3 tablespoons
- Extra-firm tofu, 4 ounces pressed
- Chopped tomatoes, 3 tablespoons
- Chopped spinach, two cups
- Ten-inch tortillas, low carb, 6 single tortillas
- Olive oil, one tablespoon
- Canned refried beans, ¾ cup
- Nutritional yeast, ½ cup
- Salsa for garnish

Directions:

1. Crumble the pressed tofu and fry the crumbles in a large skillet in hot olive oil for five minutes, stirring often.

2. Stir in the spinach, black olives, and tomatoes and cook five more minutes, stirring often.
3. Smear each tortilla with two tablespoons of the refried beans.
4. Divide the tofu mix among the tortillas and spread it almost to cover them.
5. Flip in one inch of the side of each tortilla, and then roll it into a burrito shape.
6. Lay the burritos with the open side down in the skillet and fry for five minutes on low heat.
7. Serve the burritos with salsa if desired.

Tofu Avocado Toast

Ingredients:

- 2 slices almond bread (or any other gluten-free, dairy-free bread of your choice)
- ½ small avocado, sliced
- ½ cup chives, sliced
- 4 extra firm 1/2-inch thick slices of tofu, drained and patted dry
- 2 tablespoons olive oil
- ¼ teaspoon turmeric
- Salt and pepper to taste

Directions:

1. Mix the turmeric, salt, and pepper in a small bowl and rub each piece of tofu with this mixture.

2. Heat a skillet over medium heat. Add olive oil to the skillet and fry tofu slices until golden brown on each side.
3. Once the tofu is cooked, assemble the sandwiches by toasting the bread then layering with the tofu and chives. Sprinkle with salt and pepper, and serve.

Apple Buckwheat Pancakes

Ingredients:

- ½ teaspoon vanilla extract
- 1 ¼ cup almond milk + 2 tablespoons
- 1 tablespoon ground flaxseed
- 3 tablespoons water
- 2 tablespoons coconut oil, melted
- 1 cup Royal Gala apples, peeled and finely chopped
- 1 ¾ cups buckwheat flour
- 2 tablespoons coconut sugar
- 2 teaspoons salt
- 2 teaspoons of baking powder
- 2 teaspoons ground cinnamon
- Maple syrup to serve

Directions:

1. Create an egg substitute by mixing the ground flax seeds with water. Let it rest for 5 minutes.
2. Whisk together the buckwheat flour, coconut sugar, baking powder, salt and cinnamon.
3. Mix the egg substitute with almond milk and gently fold this mixture into the dry ingredient mixture. Do not over mix the batter. Let the mixture rest for 15 minutes
4. After 15 minutes, fold in 2 more tablespoons of almond milk, coconut oil, and chopped apples.
5. Heat a non-stick frying pan over medium heat. Spread coconut oil over the surface of the frying pan with a paper towel.
6. Use a measuring cup, scoop ¼ cup of pancake batter into the heated frying pan.
7. Cook for 2 minutes or until bubbles start to form on the top. Flip the pancake over with a spatula and cook for 2 more minutes.

8. Repeat until all the pancakes have been cooked. In between pancakes, rub the same paper towel on the pan if more oil is needed.
9. To serve the pancakes, drizzle with maple syrup.

Mediterranean Chickpeas On Toast

Ingredients:

- 2 large garlic cloves, finely diced
- ½ teaspoon cumin
- ½ teaspoon sweet paprika
- Sugar to taste
- Salt and pepper to taste
- 8 slices almond bread (or any other gluten-free, dairy-free bread of your choice)
- 2 cups chickpeas, cooked
- 2 large tomatoes, skinned and diced
- 2 tablespoons olive oil
- 3 tablespoons water
- ½ cup shallots, finely diced
- Fresh parsley chopped to garnish

Directions:

1. Over medium heat, heat up some olive oil in a medium-sized frying pan. Add shallots and fry until almost translucent. Add the garlic and fry until the shallots are completely translucent and the garlic is soft.
2. Add all the spices to the pan and mix. Fry for 2 more minutes. Stir constantly.
3. Add the diced tomatoes and water to the pan. Simmer on low heat until the sauce has thickened.
4. Add the cooked chickpeas and cooked until warmed by the sauce. Season with sugar, salt, and pepper and remove from heat.
5. Serve the chickpeas over toasted bread. Sprinkle with parsley.

Applesauce Muffins

Ingredients:

- 1 teaspoon cinnamon

- Few dashes ground cloves
- 1/2 cup chopped walnuts
- 1/2 cup raisins
- Egg substitute (2 eggs equivalent)
- 1 cup whole wheat flour
- 1 cup oatmeal
- 2 teaspoon baking powder
- 3/4 cup applesauce

Directions:

1. Mix dry INGREDIENTS:. Add applesauce and stir until consistency is good, then add prepared egg replacer and mix again.
2. Transfer to muffin tins (nonstick) and bake at 375F for 25 minutes or until tests done.

Whole Wheat Raisin Bread

Ingredients:

- 5 teaspoons dry yeast
- 3 1/4 cups warm water
- 2/3 cups raisins or dates
- 6 cups whole wheat flour
- 1/3 cup brown sugar
- 1 tablespoon salt

Directions:

1. In a large bowl mix all the dry INGREDIENTS: together. Add the water and beat the mixture to make a nice thick batter.
2. Pour it into 2 greased loaf pans and smooth out the tops.
3. Cover the pans with greased plastic wrap and let it rise until doubled in volume. Bake at

400F for about 45 minutes or until a tooth pick comes out clean.

Orange Raspberry Muffins

Ingredients:

- 2/3 cup gluten-free all-purpose baking mix
- 2/3 cup gluten-free oat flour
- 1 teaspoon baking soda
- 1 teaspoon baking powder
- 1 teaspoon xanthan gum
- 1/4 teaspoon salt
- 7 1/2 tablespoons water
- 3 tablespoons flaxseed meal
- 1/3 cup frozen raspberries, crumbled
- 1/2 cup maple syrup
- 1/3 orange, zested and juiced
- 3 tablespoons coconut oil, melted
- 1 teaspoon vanilla extract

- Cooking spray

Directions:

1. Preheat oven to 350 degrees F (175 degrees C). Grease a muffin tin with cooking spray.
2. Whisk water and flaxseed meal together in a small bowl to make flax eggs. Let stand until thickened, about 5 minutes.
3. Place raspberries in a microwave-safe bowl. Heat in the microwave until thawed, 10 to 15 seconds.
4. Stir in flax eggs, maple syrup, orange zest, orange juice, coconut oil, and vanilla extract.
5. Whisk baking mix, oat flour, baking soda, baking powder, xanthan gum, and salt together in a bowl. Add raspberry mixture; mix quickly with a spatula until batter is combined.
6. Scoop batter into the muffin tin, filling each cup 3/4 full. Bake in the preheated oven until browned, about 15 minutes.

Kidney-Supportive Salads Quinoa And Vegetable Salad

Ingredients:

- 1 cup cherry tomatoes, halved
- 1/4 cup fresh parsley, chopped
- 2 tablespoons olive oil
- 2 tablespoons lemon juice
- 1 cup quinoa, rinsed and cooked
- 1 cucumber, diced
- 1 bell pepper (red or yellow), diced
- Salt substitute and pepper to taste

Directions:

1. In a large bowl, combine the cooked quinoa, diced cucumber, bell pepper, cherry tomatoes, and fresh parsley.

2. In a small mixing bowl, combine the olive oil and lemon juice.
3. Toss the salad with the dressing to mix.
4. Season with salt substitute and pepper. Serve.

Kale And White Bean Salad

Ingredients:

- 1/4 cup roasted red bell peppers, chopped
- 2 tablespoons balsamic vinegar
- 2 tablespoons olive oil
- 4 cups chopped kale
- 1 can (15 oz) white beans (drained and rinsed)
- 1/4 cup red onion, finely chopped
- Salt substitute and pepper to taste

Directions:
1. In a large bowl, combine the chopped kale, white beans, red onion, and roasted red bell peppers.
2. Whisk together the balsamic vinegar and olive oil in a small mixing bowl.
3. Toss the salad with the dressing to coat.

4. Season with salt substitute and pepper. Serve.

Spinach And Beet Salad

Ingredients:

- 1/4 cup toasted walnuts, chopped
- 1/4 cup crumbled feta cheese (optional)
- 2 tablespoons balsamic vinegar
- 2 tablespoons olive oil
- 4 cups fresh spinach leaves
- 2 medium beets, roasted and diced
- Salt substitute and pepper to taste

Directions:

1. In a large bowl, combine the fresh spinach leaves, roasted beets, toasted walnuts, and crumbled feta cheese (if using).
2. Whisk together the balsamic vinegar and olive oil in a small mixing bowl.
3. Toss the salad with the dressing to coat.

4. Season with salt substitute and pepper. Serve.

Vegan Spinach And Artichoke Dip

Ingredients:

- 1 can (14 oz) artichoke hearts, drained and chopped
- 2 cups fresh baby spinach, chopped
- 1/2 cup unsweetened plant-based milk (such as almond or soy milk)
- 1/4 cup nutritional yeast
- 2 tablespoons lemon juice
- 1 teaspoon Dijon mustard
- 1/2 teaspoon onion powder
- 1/2 teaspoon garlic powder
- 1 cup raw cashews, soaked in water for 4 hours or overnight
- 1 tablespoon olive oil

- 1 small onion, finely chopped
- 2 cloves garlic, minced
- Salt and pepper to taste
- Optional: Red pepper flakes for added heat

Directions:

1. Preheat your oven to 375°F (190°C).
2. In a blender or food processor, drain the soaked cashews and add them to the blender along with the plant-based milk, nutritional yeast, lemon juice, Dijon mustard, onion powder, garlic powder, salt, and pepper.
3. Blend the mixture until smooth and creamy. If needed, you can add a little more plant-based milk to achieve the desired consistency. Set the cashew cream aside.
4. In a large skillet, heat olive oil over medium heat.
5. Add the finely chopped onion and sauté for 2-3 minutes until it becomes translucent.

6. Stir in the minced garlic and cook for an additional 1-2 minutes until the garlic is fragrant.
7. Add the chopped artichoke hearts to the skillet and sauté for another 3-4 minutes, allowing them to become tender.
8. Mix in the chopped baby spinach and cook for a few more minutes until the spinach wilts.
9. Pour the prepared cashew cream into the skillet with the sautéed vegetables. Stir well to combine and heat the dip through.
10. If desired, add a pinch of red pepper flakes for added heat.
11. Taste the spinach and artichoke dip and adjust the seasoning with salt and pepper to suit your preference.
12. Transfer the mixture into an oven-safe baking dish and spread it out evenly.

13. Bake the vegan spinach and artichoke dip in the preheated oven for about 15-20 minutes, or until it's hot and bubbly on top.
14. Optionally, you can broil the dip for an additional 2-3 minutes to achieve a slightly golden and crispy top.
15. Remove the dip from the oven and let it cool slightly before serving.

Vegan Mushroom And Lentil Bolognese

Ingredients:

- 1 carrot, diced
- 1 celery stalk, diced
- 1 can (28 oz) crushed tomatoes
- 1 tablespoon tomato paste
- 1 teaspoon dried oregano
- 1 teaspoon dried basil
- 1/2 teaspoon dried thyme
- 1 bay leaf
- 2 cups vegetable broth or water
- Salt and pepper to taste
- 1 cup dried green or brown lentils, rinsed
- 2 tablespoons olive oil
- 1 large onion, finely chopped

- 3 cloves garlic, minced
- 8 oz (225g) cremini mushrooms, finely chopped
- Cooked spaghetti or your favorite pasta
- Fresh basil leaves and vegan parmesan (optional, for garnish)

Directions:

1. In a medium-sized pot, bring 2 cups of water to a boil.
2. Add the rinsed lentils and cook them according to package Directions:until they are tender but still hold their shape. Drain any excess water and set the cooked lentils aside.
3. In a large skillet or saucepan, heat the olive oil over medium heat.
4. Add the finely chopped onion and sauté for 2-3 minutes until it becomes translucent.

5. Stir in the minced garlic and cook for an additional 1-2 minutes until the garlic is fragrant.
6. Add the finely chopped mushrooms to the skillet. Cook for about 5-7 minutes, or until the mushrooms release their moisture and become tender.
7. Mix in the diced carrot and celery and cook for another 5 minutes until they soften slightly.
8. Add the crushed tomatoes and tomato paste to the skillet, stirring well to combine with the vegetables.
9. Stir in the dried oregano, dried basil, dried thyme, and the bay leaf to enhance the flavors.
10. Pour in the vegetable broth or water to create a saucy texture for the Bolognese. Simmer the sauce for about 15-20 minutes, stirring occasionally, to allow the flavors to meld.

11. Add the cooked lentils to the Bolognese sauce, stirring well to coat them with the flavorful tomato-mushroom mixture.
12. Let the Bolognese simmer for an additional 5-10 minutes, allowing the lentils to absorb the flavors.
13. Season the Vegan Mushroom and Lentil Bolognese with salt and pepper to taste. Adjust the seasonings according to your preferences.
14. Serve the rich and hearty Vegan Mushroom and Lentil Bolognese over cooked spaghetti or your favorite pasta.
15. Garnish with fresh basil leaves and vegan parmesan, if desired, for added flavor and presentation.
16. Enjoy this wholesome and satisfying plant-based twist on a classic Italian favorite, perfect for a comforting weeknight dinner or a special gathering with friends and family!

Vegan Avocado And Chickpea Salad Sandwich

Ingredients:

- 2 tablespoons lemon juice
- 2 tablespoons vegan mayonnaise
- 1/4 cup finely chopped red onion
- 1/4 cup finely chopped celery
- 2 tablespoons chopped fresh cilantro or parsley
- Salt and pepper to taste
- Lettuce leaves
- 1 can (15 oz) chickpeas, drained and rinsed
- 1 ripe avocado
- Sliced tomatoes
- Bread or rolls of your choice

Directions:

1. In a large mixing bowl, mash the chickpeas with a fork or potato masher until they are partially mashed but still have some texture.
2. Cut the ripe avocado in half, remove the pit, and scoop the flesh into the bowl with the mashed chickpeas.
3. Add lemon juice and vegan mayonnaise to the bowl.
4. Mix everything together until the avocado is well combined with the chickpeas, creating a creamy and chunky texture.
5. Stir in the finely chopped red onion, celery, and chopped fresh cilantro or parsley for added flavor and crunch.
6. Season the avocado and chickpea salad with salt and pepper to taste. Adjust the seasonings according to your preferences.
7. To assemble the sandwich, spread a generous amount of the avocado and chickpea salad onto slices of bread or rolls.

8. Top the salad with lettuce leaves and sliced tomatoes for added freshness and color.
9. Optionally, you can add other toppings like cucumber slices, sprouts, or pickles for extra variety.
10. Place another slice of bread on top to complete the sandwich.
11. Serve the delectable Vegan Avocado and Chickpea Salad Sandwich as a nutritious and filling meal for lunch or a quick and satisfying dinner.
12. This plant-based sandwich is bursting with creamy avocado, hearty chickpeas, and refreshing vegetables, making it a delightful and flavorful option for vegans and non-vegans alike!

Quinoa And Black Bean Fiesta Salad

Ingredients:

- Cherry tomatoes, halved
- Red onion, finely chopped
- Fresh cilantro, chopped
- Avocado, diced
- Cooked quinoa
- Black beans, drained and rinsed
- Corn kernels (fresh or thawed if frozen)
- Lime dressing

Directions:

1. In a large bowl, combine quinoa, black beans, corn, cherry tomatoes, red onion, and cilantro.
2. Gently fold in the diced avocado.

3. Drizzle with a zesty lime dressing and toss until well coated.
4. Chill in the refrigerator for at least 30 minutes before serving.

Faro And Roasted Vegetable Salad

Ingredients:

- Red onion, sliced
- Pecans, toasted
- Fresh rosemary, chopped
- Cooked farro
- Butternut squash, cubed
- Brussels sprouts, halved
- Red bell pepper, diced
- Balsamic vinaigrette

Directions:

1. Roast butternut squash, Brussels sprouts, red bell pepper, and red onion with a drizzle of olive oil and fresh rosemary until tender.
2. In a large bowl, combine cooked farro, roasted vegetables, and toasted pecans.

3. Toss with a balsamic vinaigrette dressing.
4. Allow flavors to meld for about 15 minutes before serving.

Brown Rice And Edam Me Salad

Ingredients:

- Cucumber, diced
- Radishes, thinly sliced
- Green onions, chopped
- Sesame seeds, toasted
- Cooked brown rice
- Edam me, shelled and cooked
- Soy ginger dressing

Directions:
1. In a large bowl, combine brown rice, edamame, cucumber, radishes, green onions, and sesame seeds.
2. Toss with a soy ginger dressing until evenly coated.
3. Refrigerate for at least 1 hour before serving to enhance flavors.

Shoyu Ramen With Teriyaki Glazed Eggplant

Ingredients:

- 4 cups vegetable broth
- 1/4 cup soy sauce
- 2 tbsp mirin
- 1 tbsp sesame oil
- 1 tbsp ginger, grated
- 1 cup bean sprouts
- 8 oz ramen noodles
- 1 large eggplant, sliced
- 1/2 cup teriyaki sauce
- 3 green onions, thinly sliced

Directions:

1. Preheat the oven to 400°F (200°C). Brush eggplant slices with teriyaki sauce and bake for 20-25 minutes.
2. Cook ramen noodles according to package Directions:. Drain.
3. In a pot, combine vegetable broth, soy sauce, mirin, sesame oil, and grated ginger. Simmer for 15 minutes.
4. Divide noodles into bowls, add teriyaki-glazed eggplant, and pour hot broth over them.
5. Garnish with bean sprouts and green onions.

Ginger-Sesame Shoyu Ramen With Crispy Tofu

Ingredients:

- 4 cups vegetable broth
- 1/4 cup soy sauce
- 1 tbsp miso paste
- 1 tbsp sesame oil
- 2 cups baby bok choy, halved
- 1 cup snow peas, trimmed
- 4 green onions, thinly sliced
- 10 oz ramen noodles
- 1 block extra-firm tofu, pressed and cubed
- 1/3 cup soy sauce
- 2 tbsp sesame oil
- 1 tbsp fresh ginger, grated

Directions:

1. Cook ramen noodles according to package Directions:. Drain and set aside.
2. Toss tofu cubes with soy sauce and sesame oil. Bake until crispy.
3. In a pot, combine vegetable broth, soy sauce, miso paste, and sesame oil. Bring to a simmer.
4. Add baby book Choy and snow peas to the broth, cook until tender.
5. Divide noodles into bowls, ladle hot broth over them, and top with crispy tofu and green onions.

Lemongrass-Infused Shout Ramen

Ingredients:

- 2 tbsp rice vinegar
- 1 tbsp sesame oil
- 1 tbsp fresh lemongrass, finely chopped
- 1 cup shiitake mushrooms, sliced
- 1 cup tofu, cubed
- 1 cup bean sprouts
- 9 oz ramen noodles
- 4 cups vegetable broth
- 1/4 cup soy sauce
- 2 stalks lemongrass, smashed
- Fresh cilantro for garnish

Directions:

1. Cook ramen noodles according to package Directions:. Drain.
2. In a pot, combine vegetable broth, soy sauce, smashed lemongrass, rice vinegar, and sesame oil. Simmer for 20 minutes.
3. Remove smashed lemongrass and add fresh lemongrass, mushrooms, and tofu. Cook until mushrooms are tender.
4. Divide noodles into bowls, ladle hot broth over them, and top with bean sprouts and fresh cilantro.

Creamy Avocado Spread

Ingredients:

- 2 teaspoons lemon juice
- 2 cloves garlic, minced
- Salt and pepper to taste
- 2 ripe avocados
- Optional: Red pepper flakes or cilantro for additional taste

Directions:
1. Cut the avocados in half, remove the pits, and scoop out the meat into a basin.
2. Add lemon juice, minced garlic, salt, pepper, and any desired spices.
3. Mash and blend all INGREDIENTS: until smooth and thoroughly mixed.
4. Directions:

5. Spread the Creamy Avocado Spread over toast, or sandwiches, or use it as a savory dip for vegetables and crackers.
6. Store any remaining spread in an airtight jar in the refrigerator.

Kid-Friendly Guacamole

Ingredients:

- 1/4 cup coarsely chopped red onion
- 1 tablespoon lime juice
- 1/4 teaspoon garlic powder
- 2 ripe avocados
- 1 small tomato, chopped
- Salt and pepper to taste

Directions:

1. Cut the avocados in half, remove the pits, and scoop out the meat into a mixing bowl.
2. Mash the avocados with a fork until somewhat chunky.
3. Add diced tomato, chopped red onion, lime juice, garlic powder, salt, and pepper. Mix gently to blend.
4. Directions:

5. Serve the Kid-Friendly Guacamole with tortilla chips, as a topping for tacos, or with other favorite foods.
6. This gentle and tasty guacamole is excellent for toddlers who may prefer a softer taste.

Easy Homemade Vegan Cheese Dip

Ingredients:

- 1 tablespoon lemon juice
- 1/2 teaspoon garlic powder
- 1/2 teaspoon onion powder
- Salt and pepper to taste
- 1 cup raw cashews (soaked in water for 2-4 hours or overnight)
- 1/4 cup nutritional yeast
- Water as required for desired consistency

Directions:

1. Drain and rinse the soaked cashews completely.
2. In a blender or food processor, add the cashews, nutritional yeast, lemon juice, garlic powder, onion powder, salt, pepper, and a splash of water.

3. Blend until smooth, adding additional water if required to get the desired consistency.
4. Directions:
5. Serve the Easy Homemade Vegan Cheese Dip with fresh vegetables, and pretzels, or use it as a dipping sauce for your favorite foods.
6. Store any leftover dip in the refrigerator for up to a week.
7. These delectable dips and spreads provide a blast of flavor and adaptability to any meal.
8. Whether it's the creamy richness of the Creamy Avocado Spread, the kid-friendly appeal of the Guacamole, or the savory joy of the Easy Homemade Vegan Cheese Dip, each dish provides a wonderful and healthful complement to meals, snacks, or parties.
9. Embrace these inventions for a rich and joyful eating experience.

Banana Quinoa Oatmeal

Ingredients:

- ¾ cup Almond Milk, light
- ½ tsp. Cinnamon, ground
- 2 tbsp. Peanut Butter, organic
- ½ cup Oats
- ½ cup Quinoa, dry
- 2 Bananas, ripe
- 1 tsp. Vanilla

Directions:

1. To start, place the quinoa, nutmeg, almond milk, cinnamon, and vanilla in a small saucepan.
2. Heat the saucepan over a medium heat and bring the mixture to a boil.
3. Once it starts boiling, lower the heat and allow it to simmer for 10 to 15 minutes. Tip:

The quinoa should have absorbed all the liquid in this time.
4. Next, fluff the quinoa mixture with a fork and then transfer to a serving bowl.
5. Now, spoon in the peanut butter and stir well.
6. Finally, top with the banana.

Gingerbread Chia Porridge

Ingredients:

- ¼ tsp. Cinnamon, grounded
- 1 tbsp. Maple Syrup
- Dash of Sea Salt
- ¼ tsp. Ginger, grounded
- ¼ cup Chia Seeds
- Pinch of Clove, grounded
- ¾ cup Soy Milk, unsweetened

For garnishing:

- 1 tbsp. Raisins

Directions:

1. Start by combining all the INGREDIENTS: needed to make the oatmeal in a mason jar.
2. Place the Mason jar in the refrigerator for 8 hours.

3. Stir once the porridge before keeping it for refrigeration.
4. Now, garnish it with raisins.
5. Serve and enjoy.

Roasted Balsamic Brussels Sprouts

Ingredients:

- 2 tablespoons balsamic vinegar
- 2 cloves garlic, minced
- Salt and black pepper to taste
- 1 lb Brussels sprouts, trimmed and halved
- 2 tablespoons olive oil
- Optional: ¼ cup chopped walnuts

Directions:

1. Preheat the oven to 400°F (200°C).
2. In a mixing bowl, toss the Brussels sprouts with olive oil, balsamic vinegar, minced garlic, salt, and pepper until evenly coated.
3. Spread the Brussels sprouts on a baking sheet in a single layer.

4. Roast in the preheated oven for 20-25 minutes or until the sprouts are tender and caramelized, stirring halfway through.
5. If using walnuts, add them during the last 5 minutes of roasting for a toasted crunch.
6. Remove from the oven and serve hot.

Quinoa Primavera

Ingredients:

- 2 cloves garlic, minced
- 1 red bell pepper, diced
- 1 zucchini, diced
- 1 cup cherry tomatoes, halved
- 1 teaspoon dried oregano
- Salt and pepper to taste
- 1 cup quinoa
- 2 cups vegetable broth or water
- 1 tablespoon olive oil
- 1 small onion, finely chopped
- Fresh basil leaves for garnish (optional)

Directions:

1. Rinse the quinoa thoroughly under cold water.
2. In a saucepan, bring the vegetable broth or water to a boil. Add the quinoa, reduce heat to low, cover, and simmer for 15-20 minutes or until the liquid is
3. Absorbed and quinoa is cooked. Remove from heat and let it sit covered for 5 minutes. Fluff with a fork.
4. In a large skillet, heat olive oil over medium heat. Add onions and garlic, sauté until fragrant and translucent.
5. Add the bell pepper and zucchini. Cook for 5-7 minutes until they begin to soften.
6. Stir in the cherry tomatoes, dried oregano, salt, and pepper. Cook for an additional 3-4 minutes until tomatoes are slightly softened.
7. Combine the cooked quinoa with the vegetable mixture in the skillet. Toss gently until well combined and heated through.

8. Serve hot, garnished with fresh basil leaves if desired.

Creamy Cashew Cheese Sauce

Ingredients:

- 2 tablespoons nutritional yeast
- 1 clove garlic, minced
- 1 tablespoon lemon juice
- 1 teaspoon onion powder
- 1 cup raw cashews, soaked for 2-4 hours or overnight
- 1 cup unsweetened almond milk (or any plant-based milk)
- Salt and pepper to taste

Directions:

1. Soak Cashews: Place the raw cashews in a bowl and cover them with water. Allow them to soak for at least 2-4 hours or overnight for a creamier texture.

2. Drain and Rinse: Drain the soaked cashews and rinse them thoroughly.
3. Blend INGREDIENTS: In a high-speed blender, combine the soaked cashews, almond milk, nutritional yeast, minced garlic, lemon juice, and onion powder. Blend until smooth and creamy.
4. Season to Taste: Taste the sauce and adjust the flavor by adding salt and pepper as needed. You can also customize the seasoning with herbs or spices like paprika, cayenne pepper, or fresh herbs for added depth.
5. Heat (Optional): Pour the sauce into a saucepan and gently heat it over low-medium heat, stirring continuously, until warmed through.
6. Avoid boiling to maintain the creamy texture.

Vegan Tofu And Vegetable Wrap

Ingredients:

- 1 tablespoon soy sauce
- 1 tablespoon rice vinegar
- 1 tablespoon sesame oil
- Salt and pepper, to taste
- 1 block extra-firm tofu, drained and pressed
- 1/2 red onion, diced
- 1/2 red pepper, diced
- 1/2 cup shredded carrots
- 1/2 cup shredded cabbage
- 4 whole wheat tortillas

Directions:

1. Cut the pressed tofu into small cubes and sauté them in a non-stick skillet until they are browned on all sides.
2. Add the diced red onion and diced red pepper to the skillet and sauté for another 2-3 minutes.
3. In a mixing bowl, combine the shredded carrots, shredded cabbage, soy sauce, rice vinegar, sesame oil, salt, and pepper.
4. Warm the tortillas in the microwave or on a griddle.
5. Divide the tofu and vegetable mixture among the tortillas and roll them up tightly.
6. Cut the wraps in half and serve.
7. These vegan wrap recipes are easy to make, healthy, and perfect for a quick lunch or dinner. You can also experiment with different fillings and sauces to create your own unique wraps.

Vegan Poke Bowl

Ingredients:

- 1/2 avocado, sliced
- 1/4 cup edamame
- 1/4 cup sliced scallions
- 2 tablespoons soy sauce
- 1 tablespoon sesame oil
- 1 tablespoon rice vinegar
- 1 cup brown rice, cooked
- 1/2 block extra-firm tofu, cubed
- 1/2 cucumber, sliced
- Salt and pepper, to taste

Directions:

1. In a mixing bowl, combine the cubed tofu, soy sauce, sesame oil, rice vinegar, salt, and pepper.
2. Heat a non-stick skillet over medium-high heat and add the tofu mixture to the skillet. Sauté for 5-7 minutes, until the tofu is browned on all sides.
3. Divide the cooked brown rice evenly among four bowls.
4. Arrange the sautéed tofu, sliced cucumber, sliced avocado, edam me, and sliced scallions on top of the rice.
5. Serve the bowls immediately.

Vegan Taco Bowl

Ingredients:

- 1/2 avocado, sliced
- 1 tablespoon olive oil
- 1 tablespoon lime juice
- 1 teaspoon ground cumin
- 1 teaspoon chili powder
- 1 cup quinoa, cooked
- 1 cup black beans, drained and rinsed
- 1 cup corn kernels
- 1/2 red onion, diced
- 1/2 red pepper, diced
- Salt and pepper, to taste

Directions:

1. In a mixing bowl, toss the cooked quinoa with the olive oil, lime juice, ground cumin, chili powder, salt, and pepper.
2. Divide the quinoa evenly among four bowls.
3. Arrange the black beans, corn kernels, diced red onion, diced red pepper, and sliced avocado on top of the quinoa.
4. Serve the bowls immediately.
5. These vegan bowl recipes are easy to make, healthy, and packed with nutrients. You can also experiment with different grains, proteins, and vegetables to create your own unique bowls.

Cauliflower Hash Browns

Ingredients:

- 1/2 tsp garlic powder
- 1/2 tsp onion powder
- Salt and pepper to taste
- 2 cups of grated cauliflower
- 1/4 cup of almond flour
- 1/4 cup of nutritional yeast
- 2 tbsp. Olive oil for cooking

Directions:

1. Squeeze any extra moisture from the shredded cauliflower using a clean kitchen towel.
2. Whisk together the almond flour, nutritional yeast, garlic powder, onion powder, salt, and pepper in a bowl with the squeezed cauliflower. Be sure to mix well.

3. In a skillet set over medium heat, warm the olive oil.
4. Make little patties with the cauliflower mixture and fry them in a pan.
5. Flip once the bottom has golden brown; continue cooking until both sides are browned.
6. After removing it from the pan, set it on a paper towel-lined dish to soak up any extra grease.
7. Add a dipping sauce to the cauliflower hash browns before serving.

Flaxseed And Berry Muffins

Ingredients:

- 1/2 tsp cinnamon
- Pinch of salt
- Three ripe bananas, mashed
- 3 tbsp. coconut oil, melted
- Three flax eggs (3 tbsp. ground flaxseed + 9 tbsp. water)
- 1 cup of ground flaxseeds
- 1/4 cup of coconut flour
- 1 tsp baking powder
- 1 cup of mixed berries (blueberries, raspberries, strawberries)

Directions:

1. Line a muffin pans with paper liners and set the oven temperature to 350°F, or 175°C.

2. Toast the flaxseeds in a large bowl with the coconut flour, cinnamon, baking powder, and salt.
3. Mash the bananas, melt the coconut oil, and combine the flax eggs in another dish.
4. Mix the dry INGREDIENTS: with the wet ones before adding them.
5. Mix in the berries one by one.
6. Fill up each muffin pan three-quarters to the top with batter.
7. After inserting a toothpick into the middle, bake for 20-25 minutes or until it comes out clean.
8. Before serving, let the muffins cool.

Vegan Keto Breakfast Burrito

Ingredients:

- 1/4 cup of diced tomatoes
- 1/4 cup of chopped bell peppers
- 1/4 cup of diced red onion
- 1/4 cup of shredded vegan cheese
- One large collard green leaf (or low-carb tortilla)
- 1/2 avocado, sliced
- Salt and pepper to taste
- Hot sauce or salsa

Directions:

1. Rinse the collard greens and cut off the excess herbicide.

2. Vegan cheese, chopped tomatoes, bell peppers, avocado slices, and a flat collard green leaf top the salad.
3. Taste and add salt and pepper as needed.
4. Create a burrito shape by rolling up a collard green leaf and tucking in the edges.
5. Cut in half and, if desired, use toothpicks to hold.
6. If desired, top with salsa or spicy sauce and serve.

Brown Rice And Lentils

Ingredients:

- 1 cup whole grain brown rice (brown basmati rice)
- 1 cup dried lentils
- 4 cups low-sodium vegetable broth or water
- 1 large onion, chopped
- 1 Tbsp garlic powder
- Salt to taste

Directions:

1. Preheat a medium saucepan or large skillet over medium heat. Add the onion and sauté for 2-3 minutes or until the onions are soft and begin to turn brown.
2. Add the rice, lentils, water (vegetable broth), and salt and pepper. Increase to medium-high

heat. Bring everything to a boil, then lower the heat, cover, and simmer.
3. Cook for 45 minutes or until the rice and lentils are tender, and the liquid has been absorbed. Keep in mind, depending on your appliance or cookware, the cook time may vary.
4. Remove from the heat and let sit for 10 minutes before serving.

Instant Pot Black Eyed Peas

Ingredients:

- 1 small onion, chopped
- 6 cups low-sodium vegetable broth
- 1 lb. bag of black-eyed peas
- Salt and pepper to taste

Directions:

1. Set your Instant Pot to sauté and let it completely heat up. Add in the onions and cook for about 2-3 minutes or until the onions are soft and translucent.
2. Change the setting to Manual on the Instant Pot. Add in the vegetable broth, the black-eyed peas, and lightly stir to combine everything.
3. Close the lid. Turn the venting knob to the sealing position and set to high pressure for 20 minutes.

4. Once the peas are finished cooking, allow the pressure to release naturally for 10 minutes. Then, simply do a quick release.
5. Remove the lid, season with salt and pepper, stir, and serve.

Pot Vegan Baked Beans

Ingredients:

- 1 teaspoon salt
- 1 medium green bell pepper, finely chopped
- 2 garlic cloves, finely chopped
- 1/3 cup molasses
- 1/2 cup ketchup
- 1 tablespoon vegan Worcestershire sauce (I used Annie's brand)
- 1/4 cup packed brown sugar
- 1 teaspoon dry mustard or 1 tablespoon dijon mustard
- 1/2 teaspoon chili powder
- 1/2 teaspoon smoked paprika
- 1 pound dried pinto or navy beans

- 1/2 tablespoon salt
- 1 tablespoon olive oil
- 1/2 cup finely chopped onion
- 2 cups water
- 1 tablespoon apple cider vinegar

Directions:
1. Rinse the beans and sort to remove any debris. Soak overnight or for 8 hours with 1/2 tablespoon salt, then drain.
2. Alternatively, boil beans for 2 minutes, let stand for an hour, then drain.
3. Saute onion in olive oil in the Instant Pot. Add salt, green bell pepper, and garlic; cook until tender.
4. Add rinsed beans, molasses, ketchup, Worcestershire sauce, brown sugar, dry mustard, chili powder, paprika, and 2 cups water. Cook on high pressure for 40 minutes.

5. Allow a 15-minute natural pressure release, then stir in apple cider vinegar. Season to taste.

Cajun Corn And Kidney Bean Salad

Ingredients:

- 2 cloves garlic, minced
- 1 teaspoon smoked paprika
- 1 1/2 teaspoons minced fresh oregano, or 1/2 teaspoon dried
- 1/4 teaspoon liquid smoke
- Hot sauce, to taste
- Salt and ground black pepper, to taste
- Kernels from 4 ears cooked corn on the cob
- 1/2 cup green bell pepper or other pepper
- 1/4 cup minced onion
- 1/4 cup chopped celery
- 1/4 cup diced moist-packed sun-dried tomatoes

- 1/4 cup vegetable broth, more if needed
- 1/4 cup cider vinegar
- 1 (15-ounce can) red kidney beans, drained and rinsed

Directions:

1. Combine all INGREDIENTS: except the beans in a large bowl.
2. Stir together well, and taste and adjust the seasonings.
3. Gently stir in the beans.
4. If the mixture is too dry, add additional broth to dress it.
5. Cover and refrigerate for 1 hour to allow the flavors to meld.

Arugula Lentil Salad

Ingredients:

- 1 chilli/jalapeño
- 5-6 dried tomatoes
- 3 slices whole wheat bread
- 1 big can of lentils (15oz or 400g) (pre-cooked, or cook first)
- Salt and pepper to taste
- 100g cashew nuts (about 1 cup)
- 1 onion
- 3 tbsp olive oil
- Optional: raisins, honey/agave nectar, lemon juice or vinegar

Directions:

1. Roast the cashews on a low heat for about three minutes in a pan to maximize aroma. Then throw them into the salad bowl
2. Dice the onion into fine pieces
3. Add some of the oil to the pan and fry the onion for about 3 minutes on a low heat
4. Chop the chilli/jalapeño and dried tomatoes
5. Cut the bread into big croutons
6. Add the rest of the oil to the pan and fry the chopped up bread until crunchy. Season with salt and pepper
7. Wash the arugula and add it to the bowl
8. Put the lentils in too, and mix them all around. Season with salt and pepper and serve with the croutons

Kale Salad With Grilled Eggplant

Ingredients:

- 1-15 ounce can white beans, rinsed and drained

- 2 generous cups lightly packed fresh kale, stems removed, and torn into bite size pieces (if the farmer's market doesn't have any, I purchase the pre-washed, pre-torn kale in a bag and remove any remaining thick stems)

- 5 ounces plain or garlic-flavored hummus (half of a typical carton—I use Sabra brand Roasted Garlic)

- Approximately 1/3 cup olive oil

- 8 small-medium leaves fresh basil chiffonade (stacked, tightly rolled, and sliced into very narrow slivers), or finely chopped

- 8 small-medium leaves fresh sage chiffonade (stacked, tightly rolled, and sliced into very narrow slivers), or finely chopped
- Pinch sea salt and freshly ground black pepper or to taste
- 8 fresh figs, stemmed, and sliced in half vertically
- 1/4 cup roasted and lightly salted sunflower seeds
- 1/4 cup olive oil
- 2 medium-large cloves garlic
- 1/4 teaspoon smoked paprika
- 1/4 teaspoon ground turmeric
- Pinch sea salt
- 1 Japanese eggplant, about 10 inches long, ends removed, and cut on the diagonal into 1/4-inch thick slices

- 1/2 of a large orange or yellow bell pepper, cut into 1/3-inch or slightly wider pieces
- Approximately 1/4 cup red onion, cut into 1/4-inch slices
- Optional garnish: sprigs of fresh basil

Directions:

1. In a medium-large bowl, whisk together the 1/4 cup olive oil, garlic, smoked paprika, turmeric, and pinch of sea salt. Add the eggplant, bell pepper, and red onion and toss to coat.
2. Let marinate for a few minutes.
3. Then, heat a seasoned grill pan over medium high and grill the veggies in batches for 2 to 3 minutes on each side or until nice grill marks develop.
4. Return them to the bowl they were marinating in.

5. While the veggies grill, whisk together the hummus, 1/3 cup olive oil, fresh herbs, and salt and pepper to taste.
6. Add the white beans and kale to the veggies, pour the dressing over and toss to coat.
7. Arrange the salad on a serving platter or individual plates, nestle the fig halves, flesh side up, over the top, sprinkle with sunflower seeds and garnish, if desired, with fresh basil springs.
8. Serve immediately.

Tofu Vegetable Kebabs

Ingredients:

- 2 tsp sesame oil
- 1/4 tsp red pepper flakes
- 2 cloves garlic, minced
- 14 ounces extra firm tofu, cubed
- 1 red bell pepper, cut into 1-inch chunks
- 1 small zucchini, cut into 1-inch chunks
- 1 medium onion, quartered and cut into chunks
- 1/2 cup smooth, unsalted peanut butter
- 1/2 cup hot water
- 2 tbsp. reduced sodium tamari, or soy sauce (use gluten-free tamari if you are gluten-sensitive)

- 2 tbsp. mirin (sweet Japanese cooking wine, available in most supermarkets)
- 8 ounces mushrooms, quartered (or halved if small)

Directions:

1. Soak 10 bamboo skewers in water for 20-30 minutes.
2. Combine the first 7 INGREDIENTS: in a large bowl and stir until the peanut butter is mixed in.
3. Place the cubed tofu in the sauce and marinate for 20 minutes.
4. Remove the tofu from the sauce, and then thread the tofu and vegetables onto the skewers.
5. Start a fire in your grill.
6. When the coals are nice and hot, grill the skewers for 7-10 minutes, turning several times and brushing liberally with the peanut sauce.

7. Drizzle any additional sauce over the skewers just before serving.

Braised Lentils

Ingredients:

- 1 fennel bulb, cut into 8 wedges
- 1½ cups french green lentils du puy (or brown lentils), rinsed well and drained
- ½ cup white wine (or water)
- 3 to 3½ cups simply stock
- 4 sprigs fresh thyme
- 1 sprig fresh rosemary
- Salt and pepper, to taste
- Fresh parsley leaves, for garnish
- 1 tbsp. Oil (olive, avocado, or ghee)
- 1 large onion, diced
- 3 cloves garlic, minced
- 2 celery stalks, thinly sliced

- 8 ounces baby carrots
- Crusty bread, for serving

Directions:
1. Heat a deep 4 quart saucepan over medium-high heat.
2. Add the oil and let heat for about 20-30 seconds.
3. Add the diced onion.
4. Lower the heat a bit and let cook, stirring often, until onion starts to soften and turn golden.
5. Add the garlic and celery and continue cooking for about five more minutes, stirring occasionally.
6. Add the carrots, fennel, and lentils to the pan along with the wine.
7. Let cook for a few minutes, stirring, until wine is completely absorbed.
8. Add 3 cups of stock, thyme, and rosemary.

9. Cover with a tight-fitting lid and lower heat to low.
10. The liquid should barely simmer.
11. Let cook for 40-45 minutes.
12. Check lentils for doneness.
13. They should not be mushy or too firm. Add the extra ½ cup stock, if needed.
14. The liquid should be mostly absorbed and not be the least bit soupy.
15. Season with salt and pepper.
16. Serve topped with fresh parsley.
17. Can be eaten as-is, or served with bread or as a side dish.

Polenta With Mushrooms

Ingredients:

- 1 tbsp. snipped fresh Italian (flat-leaf) parsley
- 2 tsp snipped fresh thyme
- 2 cloves garlic, minced
- 1/2 tsp salt
- 1/2 tsp freshly ground black pepper
- 1 ounce dried porcini mushrooms
- 1 pound fresh cremini mushrooms, sliced
- 1 1/3 cups chopped Roma tomatoes (4 medium)
- 3 tbsp. olive oil
- 2 tbsp. dry red wine

Grilled polenta

- 2 1/2 cups water

- 2 1/2 cups milk
- 2 tsp salt
- 1 tsp dried Italian seasoning, crushed
- 2 cups instant polenta
- 1/4 cup grated Parmesan cheese
- 2 tbsp. olive oil

Directions:

1. In a medium bowl pour enough boiling water over porcini mushrooms to cover.
2. Let stand for 45 minutes or until soft.
3. Drain mushrooms, discarding water.
4. Rinse well under running water.
5. Pat mushrooms dry with paper towels; chop coarsely.
6. Set aside.
7. Tear off a 44x18-inch piece of heavy-duty foil; fold in half to make a 22x18-inch rectangle.

8. In a large bowl combine porcini mushrooms, criminal mushrooms, tomatoes, oil, wine, parsley, thyme, garlic, salt, and pepper; spoon mixture into center of foil.
9. Bring up two opposite edges of foil and seal with a double fold.
10. Fold remaining edges together to completely enclose mushrooms, leaving space for steam to build.
11. For a charcoal or gas grill, place foil packet on the grill rack.
12. Cover and grill for 20 minutes, turning once halfway through grilling.
13. Serve hot mushroom mixture over Grilled Polenta.

Cinnamon Walnut Porridge

Ingredients:

- Whole chia seeds, 2 tablespoons
- Hemp seeds, 2 tablespoons
- Chopped walnuts, ¼ cup
- Unsweetened coconut flakes, ¼ cup
- Ground cinnamon, 1 teaspoon
- Agave Nectar
- Unsweetened coconut milk, ¼ cup
- Unsweetened almond milk, ¾ cup
- Smooth almond butter, ¼ cup
- Coconut oil, 1 tablespoon
- Banana for garnishing

Directions:

1. Blend the coconut milk, almond milk, coconut oil, and almond butter in a saucepan and simmer it over medium heat.
2. Let it simmer until the almond butter is thoroughly mixed in, then remove from heat.
3. Stir in the chopped walnuts, coconut flakes, hemp seeds, and chia seeds.
4. Stir in the cinnamon and let it sit for 10 minutes for the flavors to blend.
5. Divide the porridge into 2 serving bowls, and sprinkle on some ground cinnamon or nutmeg, and banana if you like.

Banana Blueberry Breakfast Muffin

INGREDIENTS:

- Mashed ripe banana, 1 cup
- Coconut oil, 3 tablespoons
- Frozen blueberries, ¾ cup
- Pure maple syrup, ¼ cup
- Vanilla extract, ½ teaspoon
- Oat flour, 2 cups
- Baking soda, ½ teaspoon
- Salt, ¼ teaspoon
- Ground flaxseed, 2 tablespoons
- Unsweetened applesauce, ¼ cup
- Ground cinnamon, 1 teaspoon

Directions:

1. Heat the oven to 350 F.

2. Mix the oat flour with the baking soda, salt, flaxseed, and cinnamon.
3. Stir in mashed banana, maple syrup, vanilla extract, and applesauce, mixing just until everything is blended.
4. Fold the frozen blueberries in carefully, and then let the batter sit for 10 minutes.
5. Use a scoop to place scoops of batter on a baking sheet about two inches apart. Gently flatten each.
6. Cook for 13 to 15 minutes until the edges are golden brown.
7. Let the cookies cool completely on a wire rack. Store when they have completely cooled in an airtight container in the refrigerator for no more than 4 days. Heat for 10 seconds in the microwave for serving.

Cauliflower Fried Rice

Ingredients:

- Toasted sesame oil, 1 teaspoon
- Riced cauliflower, fresh or frozen 12 ounces
- Chopped green onion, ¼ cup
- Minced garlic, 2 tablespoons
- Firm tofu, 4 ounces pressed and crumbled
- Soy sauce, 2 tablespoons
- Olive oil, 2 tablespoons
- Chopped carrot, ¼ cup

Directions:

1. Fry the chopped carrots and the raced cauliflower in the olive oil for 5 minutes, stirring often.
2. Stir in the chopped green onions and the minced garlic; fry 3 minutes.

3. Blend in the tofu and cook 5 minutes more.
4. Quickly blend in the soy sauce and the sesame oil and mix, and then serve.

Ginger Cinnamon Waffles

Ingredients:

- ¼ teaspoon baking soda
- ¼ teaspoon salt
- 1 cup coconut milk
- 1 tablespoon apple cider vinegar
- 1 ½ tablespoon coconut oil, melted
- 4 tablespoons coconut sugar
- 2 teaspoons ground ginger
- 1 ½ teaspoon ground cinnamon
- 2 teaspoons baking powder
- 2 tablespoons molasses

Directions:

1. Grease and preheat your waffle iron according to manufacturer's Directions:.

2. If you do not have a waffle iron, you can use a non-stick frying pan and make these into pancakes.
3. Add the coconut flour, coconut sugar, ginger, cinnamon, salt, baking powder, baking soda and flax seeds to a large bowl and stir well to combine.
4. In another large bowl, combine coconut milk, apple cider vinegar, coconut oil and molasses. Mix well.
5. Fold in wet mixture into the dry INGREDIENTS: and mix with a wooden spoon until just combined.
6. There will be a few small lumps which is fine. Do not over mix the mixture.
7. Pour mixture into the waffle iron and cook on medium temperature until steam stops coming out of the side of the waffle iron.

8. If you are using this batter to make pancakes, cook over medium heat until bubbles form on the top then flip and cook for 1 more minute.
9. Serve immediately. Can be stored in the refrigerator for a few days or freezer for a few weeks. Warm in a toaster before serving.

Easy Vegan French Toast

Ingredients:

- 1 tablespoon maple syrup plus more for topping
- 1 tablespoon canola oil
- ½ teaspoon cinnamon
- 6 slices of day-old almond bread (because the bread is lightly dried out at this age, it will hold its shape better)
- 1 large banana
- ¾ cup coconut milk
- 1 teaspoon vanilla extract

Directions:

1. Add peeled the banana, coconut milk, vanilla extract, cinnamon, and maple syrup to a blender and blend into a smooth consistency.

2. Pour this mixture into a shallow, wide bowl in which slices of bread will fit.
3. Heat the canola oil in a non-stick frying pan over medium heat. When the pan is hot, dip a slice of bread into the banana batter.
4. Coat both sides and place the bread in the hot pan and fry for 2 minutes on each side or until golden brown.
5. Serve the French toast with maple syrup, fruit or any other desired vegan topping.

Artichoke Spinach Quiche

Ingredients:

- ¼ teaspoon salt
- ¼ teaspoon pepper
- 1 teaspoon Dijon mustard
- 14-oz soft tofu
- ⅓ cup nutritional yeast
- 1 tablespoon olive oil
- 1 tablespoon lemon juice
- Oil spray
- 1 14-oz can artichokes, drained and chopped with any hard pieces removed
- 2 cups fresh spinach
- ½ cup onion, chopped
- 2 garlic cloves, minced

- 1 teaspoon dried basil

- ½ teaspoon turmeric

- 2 large gluten-free, dairy-free tortillas

Directions:

1. Preheat your oven to 350 degrees F.
2. Prepare your pie plate by spraying it with the oil spray.
3. Arrange the tortillas so that they cover the bottom and sides of the pie plate. Rip the tortillas in half if necessary.
4. Bake the tortillas for up to 15 minutes. Check at 5 minute intervals to ensure that the tortillas have remained in place and are not bubbling. Break any bubbles that form.
5. Heat the olive oil in a large pan over medium heat. Add onions and cook for 5 minutes or until the onions become translucent.
6. Add garlic and cook for 2 more minutes. Add the spinach and cook until the leaves become

wilted. Take the vegetable mixture off the heat.
7. Add the tofu, nutritional yeast, lemon juice, and spices to a food processor and pulse until smooth.
8. Add artichokes and vegetable mixture to a food processor and pulse 20 times or until thoroughly mixed.
9. Pour mixture into the pie pan and bake for 45 minutes.
10. Allow to cool and serve.

Cranberry Muffins

Ingredients:

- 1/4 teaspoon nutmeg
- 1-1/2 cups non-dairy milk, with vanilla
- 2 egg replacers, prepared
- 1/3 cup olive oil
- 1 teaspoon grated lemon rind
- a squeeze of juice from grated lemon (optional)
- 3 cups vegan bran flakes
- 1 cup cranberries, fresh or frozen or dried
- 2 cups flour
- 1 cup ground walnuts
- 1/4 cup sugar
- 4 teaspoons baking powder

- 1/4 teaspoon cinnamon
- Pinch of salt

Directions:

1. Preheat oven to 400 f. Lightly grease muffin tin.
2. In a bowl, mix together dry ingredients: except for branflakes.
3. In another bowl, mix together wet ingredients:. Fold bran flakes into wet ingredients:. Let stand for a few minutes.
4. Add wet ingredients: to dry ingredients:, stirring until just moistened. Fold in whole cranberries. Bake at 400 f. For 23 to 25 minutes.

Apple Cinnamon Muffins

Ingredients:

- 1/2 teaspoon baking soda
- 1 cup soy milk
- 1 packet of regular instant oatmeal
- 1/2 cup oat bran
- 1/4 cup maple sugar crystals (or brown sugar substitute)
- 2 tablespoons canola oil
- 1/4 cup unsweetened apple sauce
- 1/2 cup unbleached flour
- 3/4 cup whole wheat flour
- 1 1/2 teaspoon cinnamon
- 1 teaspoon baking powder

- 1 1/2 cups shopped or shredded peeled apples

Directions:

1. Coat 12 muffin cups with nonstick spray and set aside. Preheat oven at 350F.
2. In medium bowl combine flours, cinnamon, baking powder and, baking soda.
3. Peel apples. You can either finely chop them or shred them with a grater. In a large bowl beat together the soy milk, oatmeal, oat bran, maple crystals, oil, and applesauce.
4. Add flour mixture, medium bowl, to liquid mixture. Careful not to over mix. Fold in apples, spoon batter into muffin cups and bake at 400F for 20 minutes. Use a toothpick to test doneness.
5. Remove muffins, let cool for 5 minutes.

www.ingramcontent.com/pod-product-compliance
Lightning Source LLC
LaVergne TN
LVHW021239080526
838199LV00088B/4751